The Yinzer Manual

36 Ways to be a Pittsburgher

By
Mr. Yinzer

Dedicated to my wife, who listens to and supports all my weird ideas. I love you.

Table of Content

---·——◆——·---

Yinzer – Noun, (informal) a native of Pittsburgh Pennsylvania. 6

Food and Drink 8
   1. Drink Iron City 8
   2. Love Pierogis, Food, and Mascots Alike ... 10
   3. Frequent Church Fish Fries 12
   4. Eat at Primanti's 13
   5. Appreciate Heinz Ketchup 14
   6. Go To A Wedding Just For
   The Cookie Table 16
   7. Get Confused When You See Beer
   At A Gas Station 18

SPORTS 20
   8. Dislike Bob Nutting 20
   9. Violate Open Container Laws
   On Steelers Sundays 22
   10. Have No Idea What The NBA Is 24

11. Suffer Stages of Grief Due
To Sports Losses 27
12. Listen To A Radio Broadcast Of A
Sporting Event While Watching It On TV .. 28
13. Argue Over Which Super Bowl
Win Is The Best 30
14. Still Think WPIAL Football Only
Goes Up To AAAA 32
15. Mike Tomlin wins with Cowher's Players 33

CUSTOMS 37
16. Wear Your Steelers Jersey To Church ... 37
17. Use A Folding Chair To Mark
Your Parking Spot 38
18. Assume The "Pittsburgh Left"
Is Part Of The Local Motor Vehicle Code ... 39
19. Don't Be A Jagoff 41
20. Party In The South Side 42
21. Shop at the strip district before
a holiday meal 44
22. Constantly Call In To WDVE,
Kiss FM, THE FAN, Mark Madden 46

CULTURE 50
23. Listen To Donnie Iris, Wiz Khalifa 50
24. Lose Money At Rivers 52
25. Speak Pittsburgheese 53
26. Constantly Complain About
Giant Eagles Prices, But Still
Occasionally Shop There 55

27. Be A Member Of The
Mr. Rogers Fan Club 57
28. James Conner Can Do No Wrong 59

LANDMARKS 62
29. Ride The Incline 62
30. Proclaim the Thunderbolt is the
King of Coasters 64
31. Call PPG Paints Arena, the Igloo 66
32. Go Skiing at Seven Springs
and Hidden Valley 67
33. Frequent Pamela's Diner,
Eat n' Park, Ritter's, And Deluca's 70
34. Distinguish Between The
Two Pittsburgh Zoos 72
35. Cool Off At Sandcastle 73
36. Hold Pittsburgh and Yinzers
Close To Your Heart 75

About the Author: 77

Yinzer – Noun, (informal) a native of Pittsburgh Pennsylvania.

You are about to enter the kellerful world of what it means to be a Yinzer. While not always the most elegant and sophisticated bunch, we make up for it in charming hospitality, friendliness (as long as you're wearing black and gold), and terrible driving. Being a Yinzer isn't defined by your age, sex, or religion. Being a Yinzer is more about your mindset and attitude. As we try and pull back the steel curtain on what it means to be a Yinzer, please keep in mind there are many ways to be a Yinzer and this list is not exhaustive. Also, if you are a Yinzer reading this, you may not agree with all the opinions expressed. These thoughts are simply one Yinzer's opinions and observations. Additionally, these ways to be a Yinzer are not ranked in order of their Yinzyness. With that said, strap yourself in as we head right dahntahn to see what these Yinzers are up to.

Food and Drink

1. Drink Iron City

Iron City, not to be confused with the term the "steel city" (which is another name for Pittsburgh), is the engine that fuels the furnace of the city they call Pittsburgh. And just so we are clear, yes, we are talking about a beer. While there are many beers that call Pittsburgh home, especially with the craft beer revolution that is taking place, true Pittsburghers know there is only one beer of Pittsburgh.

Iron City was first brought into production in Pittsburgh in 1861 by a German immigrant named Edward Frauenheim. Fast-forward to 1933 with the repeal of prohibition, then PBC or Pittsburgh Brewing Company was one of 725 total breweries to survive prohibition. At the time, Pittsburgh Brewing Company was also known as Iron City Brewing Company, but over the years, the company changed hands multiple times, and in June of 2009, for the first time, Iron City was officially no longer brewed in Pittsburgh. The brewing operations moved out of Lawrenceville to Latrobe the former home of Rolling Rock beer.

Iron City, although no longer brewed in Pittsburgh, will hold a special taste on the pallets of Pittsburghers, and it is still widely regarded as the true Yinzer beer. In the past, Iron City has been part of some groundbreaking innovations. They were the first to offer a snap-top can in 1962, first to offer a twist-off resealable cap in 1963, and they were also the first beer company to print sports stars on their cans. Many Yinzers will remember Steelers and Pirates printed on cans during world championships in the 1970s. True Yinzers will admit there is only one beer of the burgh, and that is Iron City.

- ✓ **Product offerings:** Iron City (Lager), Iron City Light (Light Lager), Iron City Berry (discontinued), Iron City Mango. Additional beers are in the company's portfolio, but in

our opinion they don't count since they aren't brewed under the Iron City moniker.
- ✓ **Yinzer Exception:** Occasionally drink Yuengling on special occasions.

2. Love Pierogis, Food, and Mascots Alike

The city of Pittsburgh has a strong multicultural presence. The jobs created by the steel industry attracted all kinds of people looking to make a better life for themselves. Polish immigrants were no exception. Beginning with the Polish insurrections of 1830, there began to be an influx of Polish immigrants to the Western Pennsylvania region as other Atlantic cities saw overcrowding and higher tax rates. As of the 2000 census, approximately 8.4% of Pittsburgh residents had Polish ancestry. While this may not seem like a very large percentage, the cultural influence that the group has had on the region is profound. One of the largest points of pride and well-known influences in the city has been on its food, more specifically the pierogi. The pierogi is a filled dumpling that originated in eastern and central Europe. Ubiquitous with Poland in particular, the pierogi traveled across the Atlantic with

Polish immigrants. It has remained a culinary staple of the Ohio Valley ever since.

Traditionally filled with either potato or cheese, fillings have since branched out and are only limited by the imagination as far as the modern pierogi industry is concerned. The main player in the space on a commercial level is Ms. T's Pierogis. In fact, pierogis are so popular that even the Pittsburgh Pirates have adopted them as mascots. These mascots race during inning breaks at their home games. (As of this writing, they have the following mascot characters: Potato Pete* (retired), Cheese Chester, Sauerkraut Saul, Oliver Onion, Bacon Burt, Jalapeno Hannah, and Pizza Penny) The development of these mascots has only cemented the pierogi in the Pittsburgheeze lexicon. Primanti's has even developed a sandwich that uses pierogis instead of fries.

- ✓ **Yinzer Bonus Points:** You buy your pierogi from some super old church ladies.
- ✓ **Yinzer Gambling:** Yinzers will bet amongst their friends which pierogi will win the race at the Pirate game. Wagers will range in stakes from a few dollars to one of the stadium's overpriced beers.

3. Frequent Church Fish Fries

Fish fry Fridays are a staple of the Yinzer community. Pittsburgh has a large Catholic population. Each year, starting with the Catholic Lenten season, churches all around Pittsburgh begin to host fish fries on Fridays. These fish fries are held to ensure Catholics who traditionally do not eat meat on Fridays are able to enjoy a hot meal without any meat. Some may be skeptical of these church ladies' abilities to put together a quality meal. However, ask any Yinzer, Catholic or not, and they will tell you these church ladies know what they are doing. Regardless if you are adhering to a religious tradition or not, it's always a good time to eat at a fish fry. Yinzers have become so enamored with their fish fries that they have even gone so far as to rank the local fish fries. Now, I don't need to tell you, these rankings are a huge point of pride and debate amongst Yinzers. Is your fish fry the best? Is my fish fry the best? Surely, this list was motivated by many late-night Iron City fueled debates amongst friends trying to figure out whose fish fry was truly number one. Out of fear of retribution, no specific fish fries will be mentioned. Any non-

Yinzers reading this will just have to try each fish fry and decide for themselves.

- ✓ **Yinzer Bonus Points:** You also volunteer to help at the fish fry.
- ✓ **Yinzer Turn On:** Your significant other comes home reeking of fried fish.

4. Eat at Primanti's

Primanti's is a local sandwich shop and bar that has numerous locations around Pittsburgh. More recently, Primanti's has expanded its reach beyond Pittsburgh these days with franchises in multiple states. Their self-proclaimed #2 bestseller, the "Pittsburgher," should really be called the "Yinzer," but that is just one man's opinion. The "Pittsburgher" is a cheesesteak sandwich with coleslaw and french fries directly on the sandwich. All Primantis original sandwiches have coleslaw and fries directly on the sandwich. The "Pittsburgher" is the most popular.

Joe Primanti started Primantis with his brothers selling the sandwiches to hungry truckers. The idea was that if you place the coleslaw and fries directly on the sandwich, it is a full meal on the go. The very first store was established on 18th and

Smallman in Pittsburgh's iconic strip district. They were open from 3 a.m. to 3 p.m. every day. When Joe retired in the '40s, his family took over. They proudly ran the establishment until the 1970s when Jim Patrinos purchased the business. Eventually, a second location was opened in the heart of the University of Pittsburgh's campus in Oakland. Primanti's has since expanded its operations to include locations in PNC Park and Heinz Field. They have also established locations in many other states (Florida, Ohio, West Virginia, Maryland, and Indiana). They continue to expand their reach year by year and store by store. Primantis is a shining example of American culinary ingenuity.

- ✓ **Bonus Points:** Patrons often ask what the number one bestseller is as it is not listed on the menu. True Yinzers know the answer is Iron City Beer.
- ✓ **Yinzer Power Move:** Add one or more eggs to your sammich.

5. Appreciate Heinz Ketchup

Founded in Pittsburgh in 1869, Heinz is a point of pride for Yinzers. No true Yinzer would eat any other ketchup. Henry J. Heinz, the man who started the company, was born in America to German immigrants. At first, Heinz founded the Heinz and Noble Company, which started out by selling horseradish. However, Heinz and Noble went bankrupt in 1875, and Henry decided to start F & J Heinz with his brother John Heinz and his cousin Frederick Heinz in 1876. This is where they developed the famous Ketchup. The H. J. Heinz Company was later born when Henry bought out his two partners in 1888. He continued to grow the company until his death in 1919. During this time, he developed the slogan "57 Varieties." This slogan was an interesting choice as at the time the slogan was adopted, the Company sold over 60 varieties of products. Heinz decided to cut some of the lesser selling items to make sure the Company had exactly 57 varieties. Upon his passing, his family took over and continued to grow the company. There were the flops such as green ketchup and then the home runs such as regular ketchup. As Heinz has grown, Pittsburgh has proudly supported the company, and Heinz has stayed true to its roots with its corporate headquarters still to this day, located in Pittsburgh, PA. Yinzers are so loyal that when local amusement park Kennywood switched to a mockery of a Ketchup brand, Hunts, they drafted a petition to bring back Heinz.

Today since its merger with the Kraft Company, the resulting Kraft Heinz company is considered the 5th largest food company worldwide.

- ✓ **Yinzer Bonus:** Own and proudly support Heinz with the wearing of your Pickle Pin.
- ✓ **Yinzer Double Bonus:** You still have unopened bottles of the green and even more obscure purple ketchup in your house because you believe it is a "collector's item."
- ✓ **Yinzer Secret:** When trying to get the Ketchup out of a glass bottle, tap the 57 logo to expedite the extraction.
- ✓ **Yinzer Loyalty:** Refuse to eat at a restaurant that offers Hunt's ketchup.

6. Go To A Wedding Just For The Cookie Table

All cities have their own quirky traditions, especially when it comes to weddings. Pittsburgh is no different. Yinzers will get funny looks when they go to a wedding in Ohio and ask where the cookie table is. If you have to ask what a cookie table is, then you are truly missing out on the best part of a wedding, according to Yinzers.

In basic terms, the "cookie table" is exactly what it sounds like, a table with cookies on it. However, as we peel back the layers on this Pittsburgh tradition, we are soon to realize that there is a profound significance to the cookie table. Generally, the cookie table is composed of cookies made by family members of the bride and groom. People involved in this process will generally make their favorite cookies, the bride and groom's favorite cookies, and their significant other's favorite cookies. Participants will also get cookies made by local bakeries and cookies with designs on them, such as Heinz ketchup bottles, terrible towels, and the like.

Lastly, the best part of the cookie table is not only do you get to enjoy the cookies at the wedding, Yinzer and Pittsburgh tradition dictates that the wedding hosts provide guests with to-go boxes, so they can take cookies with them as they leave, and enjoy them after the wedding.

- ✓ **Yinzer Savvy:** Yinzers know that taking two to-go boxes is the only way to properly enjoy your post-wedding cookies.

- ✓ **Yinzer Fun Fact:** No one knows how this Yinzer tradition was started, and quite frankly nobody cares just as long as you provide massive quantities of cookies at your wedding.

7. Get Confused When You See Beer At A Gas Station

What's the first sign that you're not a Yinzer? You start asking people where the beer is at the gas station. PA, in general, has always been overly restrictive with alcohol sales, and this is something that Yinzers are all too familiar with. The last thing a Yinzer needs is to drive a few extra miles down the road to a beer distributor prior to its closing as opposed to driving to their local gas station to grab some emergency beers. More recently, some Getgo's, as well as some Giant Eagles, have begun selling beer and wine. This is generally viewed as a loophole by Yinzers, but they will not complain about it. These places sell prepared food, and technically qualify as cafés, and thus can sell alcohol. A subtle distinction sure, but hey, if it makes it more convenient for us Yinzers to buy some Irons, we are all for it.

The Yinzer Manual

Even with the additional availability of beer at some gas stations, true Yinzers take pride in frequenting their local beer distributor. Going to the beer distributor is as much a slice of Americana as being a Yinzer. The smells, the sights, the sounds, the selection; all are important nuances that gas stations will never be able to compete with. Eventually, as big money continues to ramp up the pressure on alcohol sale reform legislation something has to give. However, Yinzers will continue to fight the good fight, supporting local businesses and staying true to their communities as long as they can.

- ✓ **Extra Yinzer:** You have only ever purchased beer from a beer distributor.
- ✓ **Epic Yinzer:** You have only ever purchased Iron City beer.

SPORTS

8. Dislike Bob Nutting

While the Penguin and Steeler ownership groups are revered in the city, Pirates ownership is a different story. While many billionaire owners are more focused on winning, as they already have billions of dollars, the perception in Pittsburgh is that current principal owner and chairman Bob Nutting is more concerned with the bottom line. Nutting became the Pirates organization's principal owner on January 12, 2007, but he has controlled his family's interest in the club since 2002. Year in and year out, the organization is near the bottom of the league in payroll. The effects of which culminated in a 20-year losing streak from 1993 to 2012. The streak finally ended with a winning season in 2013, finishing second in the NL

Central with 94 wins and 68 losses. The pirates were able to beat the Cincinnati Reds in the wild card game and eventually lost to the St. Louis Cardinals in the divisional round. Outside of this bright spot, the team has been poor at best. Every time the team has a few losing seasons, the ownership will blame the manager. Ultimately, the manager will eventually be fired in an attempt to shift blame away from ownership. True Yinzers know that in order to win games, a manager has to have players to manage. Bob Nutting has not provided the resources necessary to sign competent players during his time as team owner. Now you know why Yinzers don't like Bob Nutting. Also, beer is too expensive at PNC Park.

Honestly, though, PNC Park is a beautiful park; Yinzers just wish we had a team that was as great as the stadium. No matter how bad, no matter whom the owner, true Yinzers will never fully abandon the Pirates.

- ✓ **Yinzer Fun Fact:** Yinzers evaluate and assess each other's Yinzyness by how many obscure Pirate players they can name, examples include: Jeff Reboulet, Brad Eldred,

Matt Morris, Jeromy Burnitz, Bobby Hill, and Adam Hyzdu.
- ✓ **Yinzer Tip:** Wait until right before a Pirates game to purchase tickets on a third-party marketplace. Generally, because the team is not very good, ticket prices will fall right before the first pitch as people want to unload their tickets.

9. Violate Open Container Laws On Steelers Sundays

What's better than beer and football? Yinzers think this is a very stupid question with an extremely simple answer, NOTHING. Pittsburgh has often been characterized as a drinking town with a football problem. The Steelers owners the Rooneys are highly regarded throughout the city and their late owner Dan Rooney was even named the United States Ambassador to Ireland. What running a football team has to do with being an ambassador, Yinzers aren't quite sure, but it sure does sound cool.

Steelers Sunday is an event in the city. Any non-Yinzer can easily tell if the team won or lost come

Monday morning based on the mood of the Yinzers around them. If the Steelers lose, the week is ruined and most Yinzers would contend that they would love to just fast-forward to the next Sunday, where there hopefully is a better outcome. The tailgates prior to the games are one of the best parts of attending a Steelers game. Heading to a 1 o'clock game is a very Yinzy excuse to day drink. While it is not legally true, anecdotally, Yinzers will tell you that open container laws around the stadium do seem to not exist, at least prior to game time. You will see Yinzers pissing on the side of the parking lot, beer in hand, and this is considered not only normal but encouraged behavior. So if you are visiting from another city because your friends are Yinzers don't be alarmed when you see men shot-gunning beer at 11 a.m., this just means it's football season.

- ✓ **Yinzer Warning:** Do not wear an opposing team jersey to Heinz Field. It doesn't matter if you are 8 or 48 years old, Yinzers will verbally abuse you until you cry to your mom.
- ✓ **Yinzer Bonus Points:** You take Monday off to attend a Steelers game on Sunday.

- ✓ **Yinzer Double Bonus Points:** Chug your beer right before entering Heinz field.
- ✓ **Yinzer Mega Bonus Points:** Chug your beer while being arrested.
- ✓ **Yinzer Legend:** Run on to the field during a game.

10. Have No Idea What The NBA Is

Pittsburgh is a college basketball town. This is not by choice but by requirement. Pittsburgh does not have a professional NBA team. Occasionally, Yinzers might be forced to interact with someone from Cleveland, and they might even ask the Yinzer what they think of LeBron, even if he isn't currently playing for the Cavs. A typical Yinzy response is "who the heck is LeBron" or what the heck are the "Cavs"?

Due to the fact that Yinzers don't have an NBA team to cheer for, they cheer for the University of Pittsburgh Panthers, who play their games at the "Pete" or the Peterson Events Center, right in the heart of Oakland.

The last NBA equivalent level team to play in Pittsburgh was the Pittsburgh Condors. The Condors were an ABA team that played in Pittsburgh from 1970-1972 at the Civic Arena. Prior to being titled the Condors, they were the Pipers. The Pipers played in Pittsburgh from 1967–1968 and 1969–1970. The Pipers even won the inaugural ABA championship title. Ultimately, regardless of the team name, the team never caught on in Pittsburgh. Poor attendance forced the team to fold, and this left a hole in the hearts of Pittsburgh basketball fans. This hole was filled by the Pitt Panthers.

With Pitt being the only game in town, the Panthers have thrived as the main outlet for basketball within the city. The most memorable time for the Panthers was their stint in the Big East Conference from 1982–2013. The Big East was known for its overly physical style of play and always culminated with the Big East Tournament, which was guaranteed to be an intense precursor to the NCAA tournament at Madison Square Garden. As a member of the Big East Conference, Pitt achieved a solid level of success. From Paul Evans to Ben Howland and Jamie Dixon, these coaches appeared to overachieve in an area of the country not known for its homegrown basketball talent. Undoubtedly with Pitt in a large city with no other basketball team, these college coaches had the edge when recruiting compared to other schools in a similar position.

In 2013, Pitt moved to the ACC and entered an era of transition. Gone were the physical matchups against UConn and West Virginia. Now the team would have to adapt their style against the likes of Duke and North Carolina. Ultimately after a less than memorable tenure under Kevin Stallings, Jeff Caple appears to have the team headed in a more positive direction. Only time will tell if Pitt's success on the court entices the NBA to expand into the Yinzer market as all the infrastructure for a team is already in place.

- ✓ **Yinzer Fun Fact**: Yinzers literally do not know who plays on NBA teams, and they despise the fact that ESPN even covers the sport.
- ✓ **Yinzer Fairness:** Yinzers are fiercely loyal fans, and if they were to have an NBA team, they would instantly discuss basketball as if they were the most knowledgeable NBA fans in the country.

11. Suffer Stages of Grief Due To Sports Losses

I'm sure that many cities see their fans' emotions sway with local sports teams wins and losses from week to week. Yinzers take this to new extremes. The Steelers might lose one game, be 15-1 as they were in Ben Roethlisberger's rookie year, and during that one week with the loss, fans will question if Cowher was the right guy for the job. The second and triple guessing of coaches is just par for the course in Pittsburgh. Newly hired coaches are aware of the heightened level of criticism and are just left to deal with it. The modern component is now social media. With social media, the most extreme comments are made public to a large number of people. One of Pittsburgh's morning shows, Mikey and Big Bob Morning Freak Show on 96.1, has developed these comments into a recurring segment where they highlight and read the most outlandish comments to their listeners. While Yinzers might panic with each loss, the panic is only fueled by their passion.

If you are ever left questioning how much emotion and personal investment goes into these wins and losses by the Steelers, Pens, and Pirates fans, walk around downtown Pittsburgh on a Monday morning after a Steelers loss. Every Yinzer dahntahn will look miserable and be cantankerous if you try to talk to them. Even fellow Yinzers will yell at each other, and yet none of them will take it personally. Everyone knows they are simply exercising the inner demons that manifest after a loss. Non-Yinzers, keep your head down and just mind your own business if in Pittsburgh on the Monday after we take an L.

- ✓ **Yinzer Health Concern:** When Jerome Bettis fumbled against Indianapolis in the playoffs leading up to Super Bowl XL, a man on the South Side of Pittsburgh simultaneously had a heart attack.

12. Listen To A Radio Broadcast Of A Sporting Event While Watching It On TV

Any Non-Yinzer would wonder why you would listen to a radio broadcast when you can just listen to the TV broadcast. Generally, the two do not line up due to broadcast delays, so an outsider would think this is just annoying. Yinzers know the original reason for participating in this practice was Myron Cope. "Yoi" or possibly a double "Yoi," Myron

Cope was basically the Stewart Scott of Pittsburgh broadcasting before there was even a Stuart Scott. He was known for all his crazy catchphrases and his infectious enthusiasm for the on-the-field action.

Unfortunately, Myron passed away in 2008 after thirty-five years of broadcasting, but his spirit lives on in a big way. Myron invented the terrible towel. Anyone that has been to Heinz Field knows what the terrible towel is. It is the first-ever rally towel. Originally, the radio broadcaster's idea was to tell fans to bring a towel to twirl at the games to inspire the players; it has now turned into a phenomenon. Now there is the official Myron Cope branded towel and there are iterations for all occasions. One of the most inspiring aspects of the terrible towel is that all proceeds earned from selling the towel are donated to the Allegheny Valley School located in Coraopolis. Myron's son suffers from severe autism and Myron elected to have all profits earned from selling the towel directed to the organization taking care of his son. To date, the sales of the terrible towel have helped raise over $3 million dollars for the school. It is this incredible act of charity and a "one of a kind" voice that has inspired Pittsburghers to hold Myron in their heart well after his death.

- ✓ **Yinzer Fact:** If you have ever used a terrible towel to clean or wipe up a mess, you are NOT a Yinzer.
- ✓ **Yinzer Exception:** The more beer you have spilled on your terrible towel, the more of a Yinzer you are.

13. Argue Over Which Super Bowl Win Is The Best

When it comes to Super Bowls, Pittsburghers have to argue over which Super Bowl victory is the best. While teams such as the Eagles have to cherish their single championship and Browns fans dream of the day they will win a Super Bowl, the Steelers have six championships. The Steelers won Super Bowls IX, X, XIII, XIV, XL, and XLIII (1974, 1975, 1978, 1979, 2005, and 2008). There are many arguments to be made when evaluating each of these championships. One argument that seems to occur often is the classic Ben or Terry argument. Older Yinzers especially will say that Terry is the better quarterback. He has four of the six championships and that is all that needs to be said.

Younger Yinzers will say that while Terry is a good quarterback, he would never be able to play in the modern-day NFL. Ben proponents will also point to the fact that Ben has a 64% career completion percentage and Terry has a 52% career completion percentage. Millennial Yinzers will also point to Ben's more than fifty-five thousand yards passing compared to Bradshaw's twenty-eight thousand yards passing. Younger and older Yinzers will not only argue over the quarterbacks, but they will also argue over the receivers, such as Stallworth and Swann vs. Santonio and Heinz.

This type of argument is a great problem to have. Steelers fans have so many championships, they can't pick a favorite. The real secret to these arguments is that there is not a right or wrong answer. All Yinzers are fans of Defense and don't really care about style points, as long as the team wins.

- ✓ **Yinzer Secret:** Arguing over your favorite Super Bowl win is more an exercise in pissing off fans from other cities. Yinzers will intentionally allow opposing fans to overhear this argument.

14. Still Think WPIAL Football Only Goes Up To AAAA

You might hear a Yinzer say, "Back in my day, high school football only went up to AAAA," and this Yinzer would be correct. Up until the 2016 season, high school football had been segregated into four classes A, AA, AAA, and AAAA, with "quad A" or AAAA being the schools with the largest enrollments. This is a great system and most states abide by it. This way, smaller schools with smaller enrollments play similar-sized schools that have a very similar talent pool to get players from. This allows for more even competition as a whole. There was one flaw with the system in that it was too aggregated, specifically at the top. In quad A, in particular, you had schools that were too big for AAA at an enrollment of 500, and schools that were too big for AAA at an enrollment of 1,000. This left smaller quad A schools such as Fox Chapel to play larger quad A schools such as North Allegheny. Needless to say, the smaller schools got murdered on the football field. It was more or less assault disguised as football with how lopsided some of the scores were.

Factoring all this into account, the PIAA knew something needed to change. A new scale was implemented and now PA football goes up to 6A. This more pragmatic approach will hopefully allow your optometrist's son to avoid a brain injury by the time he hits seventeen. However, Yinzers can't stand change. "Back in my day, we played all these big schools, and we beat them," an old Yinzer will exclaim. Luckily for him, nobody remembers the scores of those games to argue with him.

- ✓ **Yinzer Football Fact:** Rob Gronkowski transferred to Woodland Hills to play football there his senior year. He should have been ineligible since it is against the rules to transfer for sports in the WPIAL.
- ✓ **Yinzer Football Fact:** Woodland Hills High School has seen twelve NFL players matriculate through their program since the school opened back in 1987.

15. Mike Tomlin wins with Cowher's Players

Mike Tomlin gets a lot of credit from the outside world for being a good coach. When we say outside world, we are talking about praise from non-Yinzers. The people that love Mike Tomlin the most are generally the national media or people from outside of Pittsburgh in general. Yinzers, at every turn, are quick to criticize Tomlin. His poor clock management and awful challenge record are a few reasons why. Also, Yinzers hate the idea that he is a "players coach." "You can't be their friend," Yinzers will exclaim. "Back in my day, Cowher would have whipped those guys into shape. Not like today."

Hindsight is always 20/20. Looking back on the Cowher days, it took him a long time to break through, and there was plenty of criticism of Cowher while he was coaching. The smartest thing he did, however, was he left on a high note. He had just won the Super Bowl and the city was fully behind him. He handed the keys to a Ferrari to Mike Tomlin and told him not to crash. Many Yinzers believe with the talent that was on the Super Bowl XLIII team, they personally could have coached that team to a world championship. So, it should be no surprise when there isn't a single person in Pittsburgh that gives Mike Tomlin any credit for winning Super Bowl XLIII, and Yinzers will all agree this is justified. The bottom line is Tomlin won Super Bowl XLIII on the backs of a team that already knew how to win. Tomlin won with Cowher's players. Sure he still got a ring, but Yinzers know the truth. He won't be able to rest until he wins a Super Bowl post-Ben. Otherwise, everyone will always say he isn't that good of a coach. Right or wrong, those are the facts.

Meanwhile, Cowher is a living legend in Pittsburgh. Yinzers just wish that he would come out of the booth for one last go-around. Alas, he is far too smart for that and will coast on the accomplishment of Super Bowl XL for the rest of his life. He's no Chuck Noll, but then again who is.

- ✓ **Yinzer Coaching:** It certainly helps coaching in the Yinzer City if you are in fact a Yinzer yourself (Bill Cowher, born in Crafton, PA).
- ✓ **Yinzer Behavior:** Yinzers are much kinder to local sports coaches subsequent to their coaching tenure.
- ✓ **Yinzer Mentality:** Yinzers believe that they could genuinely coach the Steelers because they played varsity football in the WPIAL in high school.

- ✓ **Yinzer Kudos:** A special congratulations to coach Cowher for making the hall of fame. Even if they put Tomlin in there someday, we all know who did the heavy lifting to set him up for success.

CUSTOMS

16. Wear Your Steelers Jersey To Church

All Yinzers own sports jerseys and one could easily argue that the Steelers jersey is the most popular attire in Pittsburgh. The Steeler's loyal fan base has much to be proud of. The organization's six Lombardi trophies are tied for the most by any franchise as of this writing. With that sense of loyalty and pride, there starts to be an ignorance of social decorum in the name of dedication. Everyone has either participated in it firsthand or witnessed it in their time in Pittsburgh, a fan wearing their jersey in a seemingly inappropriate situation. Now, I specify church, but we have all seen it in other places as well; funerals, weddings, graduations, anniversaries, you get the idea. While people from other cities may scoff at the idea of wearing your jersey in one of these situations, true Pittsburghers bleed black and gold. No matter the situation, if the Steelers are playing, and even if they aren't, a Steeler jersey is always acceptable attire for the game they call life.

- ✓ **Bonus Points:** Wear a jersey from a past player that has absolutely 0% chance of making it into their sport's respective hall of fame. Examples include but are not limited to Kordell Stewart, Jeremy Tuman, Jason Bay, and Randal Simon.

17. Use A Folding Chair To Mark Your Parking Spot

This is a Yinzer tradition where the origins of which are truly unknown. The Yinzer who began this tradition is truly one of the Yinzer masterminds of the 20th century. What is one of the biggest issues facing any person living in the city? Finding parking. This unsung hero of the city developed a fool-proof system of reserving the parking spot immediately in front of their home to ensure other motorists would not take the space. The "system" consists of putting a folding chair in the parking spot in front of your house upon leaving.

Then, upon returning, moving the chair and parking in said spot. The craziest thing about this system is that everyone in Pittsburgh strictly adheres to it. If you move a chair that isn't yours, prepare to be accosted by a grizzled veteran Yinzer that has no time for your millennial ideals. True Yinzers do not question this system as it is simply put, an institution. No matter the amount of technology, apps, or regulations, they will never take the place of the good ole chair reserving your parking spot.

- ✓ **Yinzer Bonus Points:** Your chair is not a folding chair.
- ✓ **Hardcore Yinzer Status:** You still participate in this practice even though you do not own a car.

18. Assume The "Pittsburgh Left" Is Part Of The Local Motor Vehicle Code

This is a hot topic for Yinzers. Most non-Yinzers will have no idea what this means. The motor vehicle code gives the right of way at a stoplight to vehicles turning right and going straight. Vehicles going left are to yield to the drivers going right or straight. Yinzers disagree. Why follow a very clear law and rule of the road when it might mildly inconveniences one driver. This is a unique situation where the needs of the one outweigh the needs of the many and the many oblige. In Pittsburgh, when making a left at a four-way intersection, drivers that are going straight will oftentimes slow down and allow the person making the left to turn in front of them. The driver that is going straight will flash their lights at the driver turning left to communicate this unwritten rule of the road and that they are going to oblige. Now while many non-Yinzers might characterize this as reckless, dangerous, or just plain dumb, Yinzers will flick you off if you try and follow the normal rules of the road. They will act like you are the jerk for refusing to turn left in front of them. So, all you non-Yinzers out there, proceed with caution, and decide if you are going to make that Pittsburgh left.

- ✓ **Yinzer Bonus Points:** You forget how to drive when it's raining out.
- ✓ **You're not a Yinzer:** You have been in an accident due to the "Pittsburgh left."

19. Don't Be A Jagoff

This is a tricky one. Being a jagoff can mean a lot of things to a lot of people. In the simplest terms, for the purposes of explaining what a jagoff is to a non-Yinzer, a jagoff is an asshole. However, there is a much deeper Yinzer meaning to the term that must be considered when calling someone a jagoff. Also when traveling around Pittsburgh, you might hear someone call someone a Jag; this is simply the slang abbreviation for the term Jagoff. The Oxford dictionary describes jagoff as "a stupid, irritating, or contemptible person." They also describe the origin of the word as "1930s from jackoff, perhaps influenced by jag." Ultimately, you do not want to be called a jagoff. I don't think I need to explain that to any Yinzers, but there are many ways you can be a jagoff.

1. Be a fan of any sports team not based out of Pittsburgh
2. Explain to someone how great the city you're from is, and that city is not Pittsburgh.
3. Drive like a jagoff.
4. Drink foreign, non-local beer.
5. Leave a Steeler game early to beat traffic.

There are other ways to be a jagoff, but you get the idea. The idea being, don't do it.

✓ **Yinzer Pro Tip:** If someone calls you a jagoff and you are a non-Yinzer, you can hide in plain sight simply by calling them a jagoff back. This is the only acceptable response. If you call them a jerk or say "what?", they will immediately know you are from somewhere other than Pittsburgh.

20. Party In The South Side

Every Yinzer has had a few beverages on the South Side. There is no shortage of degenerate behavior on the South Side of Pittsburgh. Yinzers enjoy great bar specials and bartenders that don't have any concept of over-serving a patron. Yes, it truly is paradise for Yinzers. The Iron City flows like the three rivers and the Primantis is packed until 2 a.m. on a nightly basis.

The South Side is partially fueled by the college kids from Duquesne as they move out of the dorms on the bluff and descend upon the neighborhood. This dynamic makes for a unique blend of residents: college kids, old people that have lived there their entire lives, Yinzers that live and work there, now sprinkle in some homeless people, and boom there's the South Side.

Some of the bars have unique specials. For example, if Crosby scores a goal while you're watching the game at the bar; for the next couple minutes, light beers are 87 cents. Some are known for their wing nights and drafts, and some are known for their dancing. Now, the South Side isn't for everyone. If you decide to party down there, be ready to really party. This is not a place for a nice quiet evening out and having a beer or two. You are definitely going to need to take an Uber home or wind up sleeping in your car. Also, you are going to see some wild stuff. There is no shortage of fights and police interactions. If you are a non-Yinzer reading this, do yourself a favor if you decide to venture into the vast abyss that is the South Side, use the buddy system, have cash on you (the wait for a beer can be a long one with the crowds), and plan an escape route.

- ✓ **Yinzer Tip:** Some bars that are mainstays in the South Side of Pittsburgh are Mario's, Carson City Saloon, Fatheads, Primantis (obviously), Archie's, The Library, and Smokin Joes among others.

✓ **Unsubstantiated Yinzer Fact:** Carson Street is the street with the most bars in America.

21. Shop at the strip district before a holiday meal

The strip district of Pittsburgh is situated on Penn Avenue and from there, it extends into the adjacent Smallman Street. Throughout this area, there are many specialty shops, most of which are centered around food.

Some of the best food-related stores in the strip district are Wholey's, Pennsylvania Macaroni Company, Lotus Noodle, Reyna Foods, S&D Polish deli, and WFH Oriental Food Market. If one is looking for hard to find ingredients for ethnically inspired cuisine, the strip district is definitely a great place to start.

Wholey's is easily one of the most widely recognized and famous stores in the strip district. This seafood-centric store also doubles as a fresh market with other meats and fresh produce. The smell walking into Wholey's is very distinctive, Yinzers will testify to that. As you round the corner and catch a glimpse of all the fish on ice and venture further into the store gazing at the large fresh seafood tanks, you know this is the place to buy quality seafood.

On the same level if not greater than Wholey's is Pennsylvania Macaroni Company. This place is in one Yinzer's humble opinion, the Mecca of cheese. If you head down to Pennsylvania Macaroni Company on a normal run of the mill Saturday afternoon, you might see a bit of a crowd at the cheese counter. However, if you are there the weekend before Christmas, you will run into a proverbial madhouse, with bedlam around every corner. As you approach the cheese counter, pushing your way through the crowd of people, you will have to take a number. Most likely, you will be hundreds of numbers away from securing your cheese order. Is the wait worth it? Yes, yes it is. This place has the widest selection of cheese in the burgh and a very knowledgeable staff to guide you through your order. Please do all us Yinzers a favor and don't wait until right before Christmas to try and learn about cheese. Time is of the essence at the cheese counter.

Fish and cheese, what more does a Yinzer need on Christmas? There are a lot of different holiday traditions in Pittsburgh; however, shopping at your favorite spot along the strip before a holiday meal takes the cake, or might I say takes the cheese.

- ✓ **Yinzer Power Move:** Offer someone in line $20 for their cheese number, or at the very least have them order for you.
- ✓ **Yinzer Tip:** Bring cash to the strip district as many vendors are cash only. There are ATMs available in some spots, but the lines will be long for these during the holidays as other non-Yinzers will make this mistake.

22. Constantly Call In To WDVE, Kiss FM, THE FAN, Mark Madden

If there's anything that's true about Yinzers, it's the fact that they aren't usually known for their technological prowess. Yinzers love to listen to the radio as it is a relic of the well-regarded past and reminds Yinzers of a time they once knew. Within Pittsburgh, as in any other city, there are a number of very popular radio morning and afternoon shows. The main shows that Yinzers listen to are: the KISS FM 96.1 morning show with Mikey and Big Bob, the Mark Madden afternoon talk show on 105.9 the X, and all Yinzers listen to 93.7 The Fan any chance they get. 93.7 The Fan is all sports talk all the time.

The Mikey and Bob 96.1 Morning Freak Show is very popular. They love to have outrageous segments with local Yinzer living legends such as angry Italian dude or Eileen from Blawnox, both of which speak with very genuine and heavy Pittsburgheese accents. One of their most beloved segments is the "Florida Stories" segment. This segment consists of outlandish and outrageous news stories that all originate from the state of Florida. The fact that they are constantly able to get new news stories for this segment amazes Yinzers to no end. They also are prominent advocates of philanthropy, known for their annual "stuff a bus" toy drive where they encourage their listeners to bring toys to their donation location where they live up the namesake by literally filling school buses full of toys to donate. And yes, if you non-Yinzers were wondering, Bib Bob is in fact big, this isn't one of those ironic names.

Mark Madden on 105.9 the X is known for his love of professional wrestling and also English premier league soccer. He is one of the few people in Pittsburgh that can pull off liking soccer. His brash and often rude remarks to his callers are the fuel that inspires his listeners to keep tuning in week after week. The self-proclaimed "Super Genius" does offer insightful thoughts and is viewed by many Yinzers to cut through the crap and get to the point. The fact that he is not afraid to call out Yinzers for being overly Yinzy allows him to actually somehow gain the respect of other Yinzers. This is due to the fact that Yinzers are generally self-aware of the fact that they are being Yinzy unless they are in the top 1% of Yinzyness scale.

Then, you have 93.7 The Fan, which is the much less edgy, less cool version of Mark Madden. They focus more on news updates and are much more of a corporate-minded setup; at least, it would appear this way to the outside. Since Yinzers are obsessed with sports and the aptly named 93.7 The Fan talks about sports all day, this gives Yinzers something to listen to when Mark Madden is not on the air. The main DJs are Jim Colony, Colin Dunlap, Chris Mack, or the AM team; Joe Starkey and Ron Cook, the lunch squad; special guest Bob Pompeani; Andrew Fillipponi and Chris Muller, the PM team. Most of these radio men also publish written pieces in the newspaper to complement their radio duties.

Lastly, you have WDVE. WDVE is the classic rock station of Pittsburgh. They play a very consistent smattering of all the best hits of the '60s and '70s classic rock. They are known for their electric lunch with Michelle Michaels, where Yinzers will call in and request a song they want to hear over their lunch hour. They are also known for the WDVE Morning Show, which is hosted by Randy Baumann along with Bill Crawford and Val Porter. However, Yinzers will always believe that it is hosted by Jim Krenn still, even though he has not been on the show since 2011.

- ✓ **True Yinzers:** True Yinzers only listen to sports talk radio or classic rock. Millennial Yinzers might listen to Kiss FM, but part of being a Yinzer is not enjoying anything new or different.

CULTURE

23. Listen To Donnie Iris, Wiz Khalifa

Everyone knows that Yinzers are loyalists. This is no different when it comes to music. We embrace local artists as if they won a Grammy the second they get their first radio play. The original King of Pittsburgh music is Donnie Iris. Originally from New Castle, PA, he was a member of the Jaggerz and wrote the Billboard #2 song, "The Rapper." Subsequently, he was a member of the band Wild Cherry. Ultimately, he rose to the status of Yinzer legend when he embarked on a solo career billed as Donnie Iris and the Cruisers. His two main hits from this solo career are "Ah! Leah!" and "Love is Like a Rock." These two hits were #29 and #37 on the Billboard charts, respectively; however, his songs will always be #1 in the hearts of Yinzers.

Yinzers will remind you that Donnie is truly the best ever, at one point, a long time ago, Bon Jovi opened for him. This is as opposed to the other way around.

If Donnie is the King of Pittsburgh music, the self-proclaimed "Prince of the City" is Wiz Khalifa. He has far surpassed being a local legend and morphed into a nationally known Rapper and Hip-Hop Artist. Wiz's real name is Cameron Jibril Thomaz, and after moving around with his military parents, he finally settled in Pittsburgh. Appearing first on the Pittsburgh music radar with his song "Pittsburgh Sound," he followed it up with "Say Yeah," which achieved national notoriety hitting #20 on billboard's "Hot Rap Tracks." As he has progressed through his career, Yinzers began to embrace him further. What really got the Yinzy juices flowing and put him into the Yinzer legend status was his song "Black and Yellow." Homage to the Pittsburgh sports scene as all the three major sports teams are clad in the aforementioned colors. This is the song that cemented his legacy as a Yinzer artist

✓ **Bonus Points:** Listen to the Clarks and "Here we go Steelers" (as long as it is a version where "Kris Brown's Toe" is mentioned."

24. Lose Money At Rivers

While having a casino in Pittsburgh is a newer aberration for Yinzers, due to their affinity for organized sports, they are not unfamiliar with gambling. Yinzers are simply unfamiliar with legal gambling. When you go to Vegas, the dealers are extremely well trained and rarely are mistakes made. When you go to Rivers, patrons might be expected to explain the payouts a game to the dealer. This is just par for the course when you are the only casino in town. At Rivers there is less of an expectation of professionalism by the dealers and more of an expectation of patrons simply going for a night out.

There has been a large increase in gambling's popularity with the recent changes in Pittsburgh gambling laws. These recent changes allow for legal sports betting within the state of PA. This is a newer advent and has made Yinzers' wallets shrink and heads explode with excitement. Now instead of betting on the Steelers illegally, they can bet on them legally. Then shortly thereafter, in-person sportsbook popularity decreased as an online version of Rivers Casino's sportsbook has become available. With all that said, there will always be the old ass Yinzers blowing their Social Security checks at the slot machines, so don't worry. You non-Yinzers will still be able to visit the casino during your next visit to Pittsburgh.

- ✓ **Yinzer Level "McYinzy"**: Bet your entire paycheck on the Steelers to win the Super Bowl.
- ✓ **Yinzer Level "Yinzy McYinzer"**: Bet any amount of money on the Pirates to win anything.
- ✓ **Yinzer Level "Yinzy McYinzer Nutting Rooney"**: Parlay two or three of the local sports teams to win their respective championship.

25. Speak Pittsburgheese

The officially unofficial dialect of Pittsburgh has a very charming sound to it. The best way to describe this dialect is to provide examples.

The Yinzer Manual

Yinzer Word:	**Regular Word:**
Crick	Creek, Stream
Keller	Color
Dahn	Down
Than	Town
Dahntahn	Downtown
Yinz	You all
Worsh	Wash
Red Up	Clean Up
Gumbands	Rubber bands
Mantis	Primantis
Sammich	Sandwich
Yinzer	Person
Ihrn	Iron
N'at	And that
Buccos	Pirates
Stillers	Steelers
Pens	Penguins

You get the idea. Any "*own" words are replaced by "*ahn," along with the various other words listed above. There are additional examples, but Pittsburgheese is not a dialect that can be learned by reading about it in a book. The way to truly learn Pittsbugheese is to expose oneself to the local culture and experience it for yourself. Readers can head to the Sath Side or Mt. Worshington and talk to some locals to experience Pittsburgheese for themselves.

- ✓ **Yinzer Fighting Words:** Yinzers will be ready to come after you if you use the word Soda instead of Pop.

26. Constantly Complain About Giant Eagles Prices, But Still Occasionally Shop There

For years, Giant Eagle seemed to be the only supermarket in town. Sure, Kroger was in Pittsburgh years ago, but then the union threatened to strike. Kroger corporate told the workers that if they went on strike, they would close all Pittsburgh stores. The workers went on strike anyway. Kroger soon thereafter closed their stores, and the workers were out of jobs.

Giant Eagle has held its stranglehold on the grocery store market in Pittsburgh for a number of years now. They drove the smaller operators and once they were able to corner the market, they drove up their prices. Don't get me wrong, Giant Eagle stores are nice but any Yinzer worth their salt does not shop there. Giant Eagle with their overpriced flowers and curbside pickup are just a little too fancy for us true hardcore Yinzers. Real Yinzers shop at Kuhn's. Think of Kuhn's as Giant Eagle's younger dumber brother. Do they have the same wide variety of products Giant Eagle has? No, but they have everything you need and they get the job done at a more affordable price. The other reason Yinzers shop at Kuhn's is that Giant Eagle has gotten too corporate and too big. Giant Eagle reeks of corporate greed. Kuhn's still embodies and symbolizes the small town supermarket as a local chain. Giant Eagle has grown too big too fast and now some stores even hand out a map so you are able to navigate through the store as it's too big. As a proud Yinzer, I must say if I need a map to find a carton of eggs, something is truly wrong.

There are always exceptions to every rule. If you are looking for something specific or specialized, Kuhn's might not carry it. At this point, it is acceptable for a Yinzer to shop at Giant Eagle. Another situation where it is acceptable to shop at Giant Eagle is if you need beer and there is not a distributor open. Lastly, Yinzers will concede that Giant Eagle much like Arby's has "the meats" and if you are looking for a cut of beef to serve when company is coming over then that is an acceptable exception as well. You can shop at Giant Eagle for these reasons as a Yinzer.

- ✓ **Yinzer Question:** What if I live right next to a Giant Eagle, and I have a high level of income? Can I then shop at Giant Eagle?
- ✓ **Yinzer Answer:** Absolutely not, a real Yinzer still shops at Kuhn's and then spends the savings on sports tickets and Iron City beer.

27. Be A Member Of The Mr. Rogers Fan Club

Fred Rogers is not only a Yinzer icon, but he's also an American icon. He was determined to make sure that children knew to be kind to themselves and to treat people with kindness. His children's series *Mr. Rogers' Neighborhood* ran for thirty-three years (1968-2001) on PBS and was a TV staple for a generation. From Mr. McFeely the lovable mailman character, to the series on how things are made, to the land of make-believe, to his iconic red trolley, his program set the tone for children's programming for decades to come. The program was also known for tackling some more difficult situations that kids are forced to deal with, such as divorce and death.

Mr. Rogers was also known for his very iconic look. He would always change his shoes at the beginning of each episode while singing his lovable theme song "Won't You Be My Neighbor." He eventually also developed a classic flipping of his shoe motion, from one hand to the other. He also would take off his jacket and put on a more casual sweater.

All Yinzers love him, and he was a Pittsburgher through and through. The recent release of the Tom Hanks movie *Will You Be My Neighbor* only rekindled the love for Fred Rogers locally and nationally.

Known for his authentic kindness, Fred Rogers embodies what it means to be a Pittsburgher and a good person. His memory will always live on through his work and the lessons that he has passed on to generations of children through the message of his television show. Sadly, Mr. Rogers passed away at the age of seventy-four, due to stomach cancer in 2003.

In 2009 a statue of Mr. Rogers was erected on the North Shore of Pittsburgh. Often referred to as the "Mr. Rogers Statue," the official title is "Tribute to Children" to acknowledge his impact on America's youth. It was built at a cost of $3 million and his image sits at almost 11 feet tall. It is a touching reminder of Mr. Rogers and a welcome fixture of the North Shore.

28. James Conner Can Do No Wrong

James Conner is the GOAT. He is the best, and if you disagree, then you can get the heck out of Pittsburgh "cause you ain't no Yinzer." James Connor, adopted son of Pittsburgh by way of Erie, PA, played at Pitt. Conner broke Tony Dorset's bowl game rushing record in his freshman campaign as he rushed for 229 yards in the Little Cesar's bowl. He won the ACC offensive player of the year in his sophomore year. He crushed the competition. During his junior year, he tore his MCL and while recovering was diagnosed with cancer, Hodgkin's

Lymphoma. He faced immeasurable adversity right before he was poised to head to the NFL. A mentally weak person would have given up, but not James. He rose to the challenge, and he decided that his attitude would be his guide. As he went through chemo, he soldiered on and battled with the heart of a champion. Ultimately, he was able to beat his battle with cancer and return to the football field. During his senior season, he bounced back and had a great campaign, especially considering all he had been through. He was even able to help Pitt beat Penn State at Heinz Field in an instant classic of a game.

With all these great accomplishments, there was only one fitting beginning to the James Conner NFL saga. He was drafted in the third round (105) overall by none other than the hometown Pittsburgh Steelers. James was going to stay in a city that already knew him as a player but even more so as a person. That's why Yinzers immediately rushed out to buy his jersey. Yinzers recognized not only the football ability of the young man but recognized his character as well. Before he even played a down for the Steelers, he will forever be a GOAT. He is number thirty in your program but number one in your hearts.

- ✓ **Yinzer Warning:** If you are overheard talking smack on James Conner in Pittsburgh, the closest Yinzer will attempt to fight you.
- ✓ **Yinzer Note:** James Conner's jersey was the number one jersey sold in the NFL for a period of time after he was drafted. This is highly unusual for a third-round pick, but then again James Conner is no ordinary football player.

LANDMARKS

---

29. Ride The Incline

The incline is a relic of Pittsburgh's rich and historic past. With Pittsburgh's steep hills, there were numerous inclines or cable cars attached to the hillsides surrounding Pittsburgh. This was a convenient way for workers to get down to the mills below. Now there are two inclines left functioning in the city. The Duquesne Incline and the Monongahela (Mon) Incline.

The DuquesneIncline opened in 1877, and the track is a total of 800 feet long, ascending 400 feet at a 30-degree angle. The Duquesne Incline has been under the operation of a nonprofit since 1963 and has remained a relic of the city's beleaguered but iconic past through today.

The Monongahela Incline was built around the same time in 1870. The Monongahela or affectionately abbreviated Mon Incline is the longest continuously operating funicular in the United States.

All the inclines in the Pittsburgh area were originally powered by steam engines. Then as technology advanced, they were converted to be powered by electricity. These two inclines are all that remains of the 17 inclines originally built in Pittsburgh during the latter part of the 19th century. As one can imagine, cars are a much more efficient way to travel up and down and through the hills of western Pennsylvania.

There are also numerous lookout points after ascending to the top of the incline track on Mt. Washington. These are located on the aptly named "Grandview Avenue." Yinzers are quick to take advantage of these great views.

- ✓ **Yinzer Facebook Tip:** Get a profile pic at the top of Mt. Washington.

30. Proclaim the Thunderbolt is the King of Coasters

Every Yinzer loves Kennywood. Most Yinzers have fond memories of school picnic day where you would have the day off from school just to go to Kennywood. From the potato patch fries to the first ride on the Jack Rabbit to playing the guess your weight game, there is no shortage of entertainment at Kennywood.

Looking back at the history of the park itself, it wasn't always an amusement park. It began as a large orchard called Kenny's Grove, a popular picnic spot for families. It then eventually became a trolley park that opened in May of 1899. Over the years, the park evolved from a popular picnic spot with some old school amenities to a juggernaut of an amusement park. Kennywood has seven roller coasters (The Jack Rabbit, Racer, Thunderbolt, Exterminator, Phantom's Revenge (formerly the Steel Phantom), The Sky Rocket, and Steel Curtain). Now, while there may be seven roller coasters at Kennywood, ask any true Yinzer what their favorite roller coaster is. There are only a few acceptable answers, which are: the Jackrabbit, Racer, Thunderbolt, Steel Phantom, and the Pippen. The key thing to keep in mind with these potential answers is technically two of these roller coasters no longer exist. The Steel Phantom was renovated and converted to Phantom's Revenge after the 2000 season. The Pippen roller coaster was rebuilt into the Thunderbolt in 1968.

The most popular choice for favorite roller coaster among Yinzers is likely to be the Thunderbolt. Yinzers will be quick to remind you non-Yinzers that the Thunderbolt is the "King of Coasters." Lest you forget that the Thunderbolt was named the #1 roller coaster in America by the New York Times in 1974. As far as Yinzers are concerned, it is still 1974, and the Thunderbolt is still number #1.

- ✓ **True Yinzer:** You can quote lines and facts from the "Kennywood Memories" VHS tape.
- ✓ **Yinzer Status Symbol:** Not only have you ridden the Sky Coaster, but you have also pulled the ripcord.
- ✓ **Yinzer Legend:** Your honeymoon was at Kennywood park.

31. Call PPG Paints Arena, the Igloo

This item could easily be covered in the Pittsburgheese section of this manual; however, we need to give credit where credit is due. The Igloo, as it was affectionately nicknamed, was built in 1961 and was originally named the Civic Auditorium. Soon thereafter, the name was changed to the Civic Arena. The original intent was for the arena to be used by the Pittsburgh Civic Light Opera. The distinguishing feature of the arena was that the roof retracted and opened to expose the arena to the open air. This arena was the first of its kind to have this feature, in what seems to be a more common occurrence with arenas built today. Mellon Financial purchased the naming rights to the building in 1999, and it was thus renamed the Mellon Arena. Many Yinzers continued to call the arena the Civic Arena and then once the naming rights expired in 2010, the official name reverted back to the Civic Arena.

The Civic Arena saw three Stanley Cup championships, including a back to back run with Lemieux at the helm. It saw the birth of Crosby's NHL career and countless other concerts and events. The Civic Arena was demolished in the name of progress in September 2011. Now in its place, there are parking spots. The old Civic Arena site is adjacent to the now PPG Paints arena (Previously Consol Energy Center). However, all Yinzers still call the new arena the Igloo or Civic Arena regardless of what large corporations want them to call it.

- ✓ **True Yinzer:** You protested to have the Civic Arena declared a historic landmark to protect it from demolition.
- ✓ **Yinzer Destination:** A great place that Yinzers like to frequent before Pens games is the Souper Bowl bar. They have great beer specials before games and a bubble hockey machine.

32. Go Skiing at Seven Springs and Hidden Valley

Yinzers are not always the most athletic people. However, they are always ready to participate in a pseudo sporting event as long as they can drink while participating. This can be seen very prominently at Seven Springs or Hidden Valley. These locations are more of an excuse to party and drink while dangerously flying down a mountain at high

The Yinzer Manual

rates of speed rather than a resort. The one good thing about this is that when compared to the Rocky Mountains, the Appalachians are puny. This allows Yinzers to have a fighting chance when flinging themselves into the great white yonder.

Yinzers will trek up to the mountain on the weekends and always will make sure to stock up at the local beer distributor on the way. They will attempt to ski for a few runs then make an excuse to head back to the cabin, so they can resume their games of beer pong. This is especially true for high school and college-age kids as they use the environment to their advantage. Many people will store their alcohol outside on their porches as the natural air temperature acts as a refrigerator. No need to take up unnecessary fridge space with all your beer. As this beer sits on the porch, college kids, under the cover of darkness, pounce on the opportunity to snag some beer from their unsuspecting victims. Many Yinzers, however, remember what it was like to be underage trying to score beer and they will chalk it up to the cost of doing business and by business, I mean partying up on the mountain.

The main thing that all Yinzers know, you still

have to keep an eye out for the ski patrol. Buzzkills on skis, they are looking to thwart your good time and make sure to never forget the time they caught you with a light beer on the slopes. From one experienced Yinzer to another, do yourself a favor and invest in a CamelBak. It makes carrying a beer on the slopes much easier and convenient. Plus, there is no trash to worry about once you finish your beer with a CamelBak. So, it is environmentally friendly and a much better option compared to throwing cans off the lift.

- ✓ **Yinzer Disclaimer:** We do not condone drinking and skiing, but we know that Yinzers will do it anyway, even though it is a very high-risk proposition.
- ✓ **Yinzer's Being Pissed Off:** Yinzers are pissed off now that Bob Nutting (also the owner of the Pittsburgh Pirates) owns both Seven Springs and Hidden Valley. Now in addition to having a monopoly on baseball in Pittsburgh, he also has a monopoly on skiing in the region. He can now charge whatever he wants and there isn't much that can be done about it.

- ✓ **Yinzer Safety:** During the winter, remember to always wear a helmet when skiing at Seven Springs or Hidden Valley. During the summer, beware the alpine slide and be careful you don't get thrown off going too fast.

33. Frequent Pamela's Diner, Eat n' Park, Ritter's, And Deluca's

We all know that every city has its own mainstay classic diners. I'm not saying Pittsburgh is any different or better in this regard. It's more about knowing which diners are the local go-to's. Eat n' Park, "The place for smiles," is similar to a Bob Evans or Denny's with one key distinction: they have the smiley face cookie. This is literally an approximately 5 inch in diameter cookie with a smiley face on it. Over the years, they have developed their brand around this cookie. It distinguishes their establishment and has become a de facto logo of sorts. The food is fairly average but it doesn't hurt to support local businesses right? Also, they have a salad bar, which is their other inflection point of uniqueness.

Now, there are also some other non-chain diners in Pittsburgh that one must visit. These are Pamela's, Deluca's, and Ritter's. They are all very similar in nature. Old school or some might say original decor and a classic simplistic menu. They are exactly what you might expect. The waitresses have been there longer than you have been alive and somehow can easily out-hustle an in-shape twenty-year-old when it comes to refilling coffee and running food. The food is what you would expect from any consistent mainstay diner with Deluca's being known for their exceptionally large pancakes.

- ✓ **Yinzer Warning:** If you are a non-Yinzer and would like to try and eat at Pamela's or Deluca's in the strip district, be prepared to wait a good while for a table. Also, be prepared to have to wait outside if during the winter months as the line can extend outside the establishment from time to time.
- ✓ **Yinzer Requirement:** Yinzers always get a smiley face cookie when eating at Eat n' Park after church.

34. Distinguish Between The Two Pittsburgh Zoos

Non-Yinzers must be warned about the Pittsburgh Zoo. In Pittsburgh, the zoo can take on two different meanings. The first and most obvious is the literal interpretation.

The Pittsburgh Zoo and PPG Aquarium are located in the historic Highland Park neighborhood of Pittsburgh. The seventy-seven-acre zoo houses over four thousand animals. These animals represent 475 species of which twenty are considered threatened or endangered. The zoo itself opened on June 14, 1898, and was originally called the Highland Park Zoo. Over the years, many improvements have been made and in the year 2000, the Aqua Zoo portion of the zoo was renovated at the cost of $17.4 million and renamed the PPG Aquarium. Known for their kid-friendly atmosphere and section of the zoo specifically designed for kids, the zoo is a great place to take the family.

The second, the Oakland Zoo, is the student section of fans at the Peterson Events Center, where the University of Pittsburgh Basketball team plays. Not too far from the actual zoo, the student section adopted the name as they were known for their rowdy fandom and loyalty. Their enthusiasm for the basketball team is wild and thus the zoo moniker is deemed appropriate. The Peterson Events Center opened in 2002 and the student section "The Oakland Zoo" has been a mainstay ever since. The Pete was even named college basketball's toughest place to play by *Sports Illustrated* in 2006.

- ✓ **Yinzer Tip:** Every Yinzer knows the polar bear exhibit is the best.
- ✓ **Yinzer Tip:** Every Yinzer knows the old Big East conference was the best basketball conference.

35. Cool Off At Sandcastle

On a rare hot summer's day in Pittsburgh, what is one to do? Yinzers will consider heading on down to Sandcastle water park in West Homestead of course. Sandcastle is the only waterpark in Pittsburgh that I'm aware of, which makes sense considering Pittsburgh is in the northeast and is known as statistically the cloudiest city in America. Therefore, it would make sense that there aren't many outdoor water park options. If a Yinzer really wants to experience the water, the three rivers have plenty to offer. Although, Yinzers know to only go swimming further upstream to avoid swimming in the cesspool around the stadiums.

Sandcastle was originally built by Kennywood Entertainment, the same company that owned Kennywood amusement park at the time and first opened its doors to patrons in 1989. Located on a sixty-seven-acre site sitting right along the Monongahela River, the park is now owned by Parques Reuinods, which is the same company that purchased Kennywood Entertainment. There are fourteen waterslides and seven swimming pools.

Sandcastle, in more recent years, has been less of an attraction for Yinzers. The cleanliness has been lacking, and it leaves something to be desired. Their admission prices reflect the perceived value of their park with unlimited summer passes as low as sixty dollars as of the time of writing. Touted as the "Best Water Park in Pittsburgh," this Yinzer notes that it is easy to be the best if you are the only one.

- ✓ **Yinzer Loyalty:** Only the Yinziest of Yinzers will go to Sandcastle on a regular basis. Ultimately, the overall inconvenient location and the fact that Pittsburgh is not in a favorable climate for a water park causes Sandcastle to have limited popularity.
- ✓ **Yinzer Bonus Points:** You try to carry in a twenty-four pack of Irons to chug while going down the slides.

36. Hold Pittsburgh and Yinzers Close To Your Heart

I have outlined plenty of ways to be a Yinzer. Some are more outlandish and hyperbolic than others. Some are factual. Some are funny. Some are serious. While the previously stated ways to be a Yinzer are a good reference point, I think the one defining characteristic of a Yinzer is their unbreakable bond with their fellow Yinzer and the kindness they are willing to show one another. It is this kindness that is forged from the blue-collar roots of the city. This shapes the image of what it means to be a Yinzer. And even though Pittsburgh continues to change and develop, the heart and soul of the city remains.

The Yinzer Manual

Stay Yinzy Pittsburgh, and be kind to one another.

About the Author:

Mr. Yinzer has been a Pittsburgher and Yinzer his entire life. He was born and raised in Indiana Township, PA, and currently resides in Shaler Township. He has a deep affinity for the Steel City and looks forward to raising his family in the Burgh. He wrote this book based on his own observations and experiences throughout Pittsburgh attending Duquesne University, and time spent working downtown. He is a first-time author, and it was his passion for the city that he calls home that compelled him to write a very candid and honest guide on how to be a Yinzer. He hopes you enjoy the opinions expressed here and that you don't take life too seriously.

Made in the USA
Middletown, DE
18 December 2022